Three Liminal Dialogues on Serotonin, Mosby and Luther

~.~

Bryan W. Brickner

Ew Publishing

Three Liminal Dialogues on Serotonin, Mosby and Luther

Bryan W. Brickner

Ew Publishing

ISBN:9781978279094

Made in the Usurped States of America.

Contents

*And whoever is patient and
forgiving, these most surely are
actions due to courage.*

The Counsel ~ XLII #43

Liminal

Liminal relates to a transitional or initial stage of a process.

Something liminal occupies a position at, or on both sides of, a boundary or threshold.

The word originated in the late 19th century from Latin limen, limin- 'threshold' + -al.

Bryan W. Brickner
Vandalia MI
November 2017

1

Sarah and Molly and FAKE News

** FAKE News correspondent Molly Role interviews Sarah Tonin about electricity and the 1977 book, The Ion Effect.*

"Molly?"

"Yes."

"I'm Sarah."

"Hi!"

"Nice to meet you."

"You too, and thanks for the interview."

"Sure, I love science Molly and, well, your reputation precedes you."

"FAKE News?"

"Everyone is asking for you."

"Yeah, we're hot right now."

"*Freakily Already Knowing Everything*."

"That's us, which is why we contacted you."

"About serotonin and electricity."

"FAKE News is reporting on the 1977 book *The Ion Effect: How Air Electricity Rules Your Life and Health*, written by Fred Soyka with Alan Edmonds."

"Yes."

"We want to retell the story of health and electricity found in the book; specifically, the ratio of positive protons to negative electrons in our air.”

“It’s quite a book Molly.”

“Dated.”

“Timely in ‘77.”

“Of course, just in reading it now, 40 years on, the science is old.”

“The knowledge isn’t.”

“We don’t think so either Sarah, not at FAKE News: tell me about Soyka.”

“He moved from New York City to Geneva in 1960; there he gets a cold that becomes chronic; his gall bladder is blamed and a doctor wants to remove it. He visits New York City and his symptoms suddenly go away; when he gets back to Geneva he tells the doctor his gall bladder is staying where it is.”

"Nice."

"Another doctor suggests it might be 'something electrical' in the Geneva air causing his illness."

"And was there?"

"There was: *The Ion Effect* follows Soyka's health journey via three discoveries."

"Go ahead."

"First, imbalances in the natural electrical charge of the air makes us sick."

"True."

"Second, ionization does not affect everyone in the same ways."

"Okay."

"Third, human activity often makes the air just as electrically sick as nature."

"That's the big one."

"Our serotonin system is the key to the big one."

"In this century – oh, excuse me, *textus-interuptus*."

"Sure."

"I gotta go Sarah: perhaps you can join me?"

"Sweet! What's up?"

"President just tweeted about us again."

"Freaky."

"We'll talk more later about serotonin and ions, okay?"

"Sure Molly – and you're getting lots of texts."

"There's no rest in being FAKE my friend."

"Word."

2

Gus and Johnny and Mosby's Gettysburg

** The spirits Gus Kotka and Johnny Reb discuss John Mosby's Gettysburg while journeying to end the representation usurpation.*

"Tell me about Gettysburg Johnny."

"Where were you?"

"Mississippi with the 99th Indiana, Vicksburg campaign."

"So you know how 1863 was shaping up then."

"Big year: the Union was getting it together and it looked like trouble for the Confederacy."

"You got it."

"And then Vicksburg fell and Gettysburg happened."

"Basically at the same time."

"So Reb, what was Gettysburg about?"

"What it was and what it became are two different things Gus."

"What do you know of the after of Gettysburg Reb?"

"Lots."

"Like?"

"Mosby."

"*The Gray Ghost*?"

"You've heard of him?"

"Soldiers talk."

"True."

"Mosby understood flexibility and fulcrums create opportunity."

"Quite the analysis."

"We had lots of time on our hands Reb, you know, and Mosby's partisans were big camp talk until, until I got killed."

"Eleven August 1864."

"Did Mosby make it through the war?"

"Yes; it was after the war though that he got in trouble with other Johnny Rebs."

"About what?"

"The war."

"Like?"

"Grant and Gettysburg."

"Mosby and Grant?"

"They became friends post-war."

"Wow."

"Something like 'Wow' is what many former Confederates, and even fellow Johnny Rebs, thought."

"I can see that being an issue."

"Mosby worked a federal job."

"Oh my."

"He even represented the US in Hong Kong."

"Talented Johnny Reb."

"Lawyer."

"His partisan nature: and Gettysburg?"

"Mosby wrote, 'Deception is the ethics of war.'"

"True words."

"They're from *Mosby's Memoirs* and that's where he talks of Gettysburg."

"When did Mosby's book come out?"

"In 1917: he passed in 1916, Memorial Day."

"Memoirs 'eh?"

"Tells some of the tales you might know from camp talk."

"And Gettysburg?"

"Do you know what a '*philippic*' is?"

"Something Phil did that was epic?"

"Somewhat."

"What then?"

"Political tirade."

"Insulting."

"A philippic would be a speech against someone's character."

"Impugning."

"Yes: in 1896, one of Lee's staff officers gave a philippic against General Jeb Stuart."

"Blaming Stuart? What for?"

"Disobeying orders."

"More than 30 years later?"

"Yes."

"What did Stuart say in response?"

"Stuart died from combat wounds in 1864 like you did, only a few months before."

"So Mosby spoke for Stuart?"

"More than that. Mosby was a witness, someone who could counter the philippic: he was with

General Stuart when the disputed orders arrived from Lee."

"Mosby was with Stuart?"

"He was scouting for Stuart's cavalry and found a way around the federal army – Hooker's at the time."

"The orders? What did they say?"

"Lee wanted to divide his cavalry so as to have some on both wings, left and right."

"Sounds good."

"Lee gave Stuart discretion; he could pass through the Confederate lines, which were busy, or try, if practicable, to pass between Hooker's army and Washington DC."

"On a clock, where were Stuart and Mosby?"

"Six o'clock, and they had to go to twelve."

"So Lee gave Stuart the discretion to choose which route would be best?"

"Yes."

"Which route did Stuart choose?"

"Mosby found a way through Hooker's line, reported the intelligence to Stuart, who then gave the orders to proceed from six to twelve via the right side of the clock."

"Counterclockwise."

"Which placed Stuart's cavalry between Hooker and DC."

"Broke their lines of communication."

"Yes, and took lots of plunder."

"What was the philippic about? The tirade?"

"Members of Lee's staff rewrote the story and pointed to Stuart (and thus Mosby) for not keeping Lee informed of movements by the Union Army."

"Twisted the facts to fit *their* story."

"Mosby caught them though."

"How? His word wouldn't be enough against Lee's staff officers?"

"Mosby tracked down Lee's order book at the archives in DC, and found a copy of the order allowing Stuart discretion to choose which route."

"Busted."

"He taught 'em, though it didn't stop 'em Gus."

"Why?"

"Nostalgia."

"Sounds like a lost cause Reb."

"True."

"Not Mosby though."

"No: he rebelled and came back."

"That's what Grant saw."

"Mosby and Grant understood coming back, the good in that."

"Lee's staff officers: they were Johnny Rebs too."

"You see my complications Gus."

"Just giving witness."

"Agreed."

"Thanks for Mosby Reb!"

"You're welcome Yank!"

3

Martin and Jackie and the Pope

** Ex-communicant Martin Luther meets Jacqueline Kennedy Onassis moments before their meeting with the Pope.*

"Jackie?"

"Martin? Hello!"

"Guten tag!"

"You too."

"This is nice."

"Our meeting with the Pope?"

"Perhaps: I meant meeting you Jackie."

“Oh.”

“I read your backgrounder: you’re an achiever.”

“Thank you Martin.”

“Tell me about the United States of America?”

“It’s part of what you knew as the New World.”

“Columbus and the others.”

“Yes.”

“And President Kennedy?”

“John Fitzgerald Kennedy.”

“He was assassinated?”

“Yes.”

“You were there?”

“Wore his blood.”

"Peace."

"He was Catholic."

"And the United States?"

"Then, about 70 percent Protestant; now, more like 50 percent."

"Lutherans?"

"Many denominations Martin."

"Many?"

"Lots."

"How many?"

"Hundreds."

"Denominations of Christ?"

"Last time I checked."

"Unbelievable."

"Martin, you had something to do with that."

"That was years ago."

"Five hundred to be exact."

"Time flies Jackie."

"And things change."

"How so?"

"You knew a world ruled by coin and force."

"Power."

"And you Martin advanced a new creation to power."

"I did? … What?"

"They call it 'ego.'"

"Ego ranks with coin and force?"

"Can even own them."

"*Mein Gott.*"

"It's only so understandable."

"Is ego soul?"

"Part."

"And part not."

"Which is why Master Blaster -"

"- *What?*"

"Master Blaster."

"*Gott?*"

"Yes."

"Is that an American thing to call *Gott?*"

"No, just around the shop."

"Mediation?"

"Right."

"So in Mediation you refer to *Gott* as Master Blaster?"

"We try to keep it light."

"I see."

"You and the Pope are the heavies."

"Which is why we're here."

"Yes."

"Do you think we have a chance?"

"Don't bring up the Anti-Christ bit."

"I can't take it back."

"You don't have to."

"I don't? No recanting?"

"Not necessary."

"Why?"

"Master Blaster."

"What about the Pope?"

"That's for the Pope and Master Blaster."

"So it's not about me and the Pope?"

"It never was, was it Martin?"

"Master Blaster decides."

"*Ready?*"

"Five hundred years ready."

"Faith."

"Thank you Jacqueline."

"You too Martin."

"Shall we?"

"Let's."

(Poof.)